"King of the Sunset Strip: Volume Two"

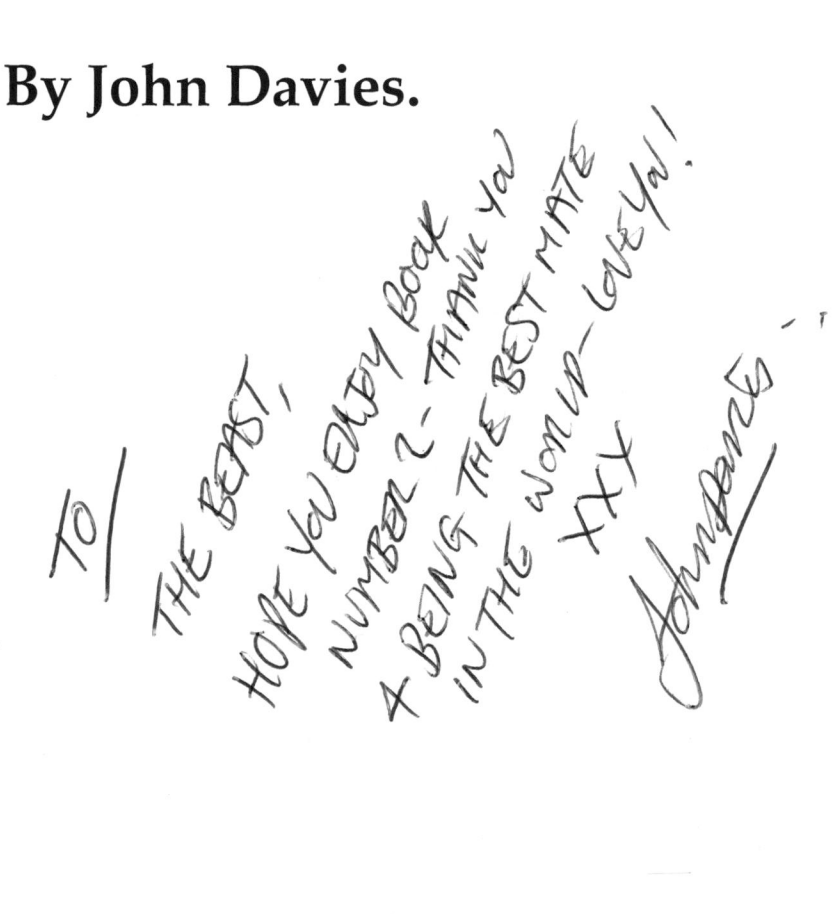

By John Davies.

COPYRIGHT JOHN DAVIES 2017 ©

All rights reserved. No part of this publication may be reproduced or transmitted in any form or by any means without permission of the author of the individual work.

Other books by John Davies.

King of the Sunset Strip.

"Dedicated to Cooper & Carter Davies, as always".

Punching Out / Checking In.

The silent tick tock of the imaginary hand,
Hitting the hour number.
Should have ended this sooner than planned,
But life always has a way of slowing us down,
When we least expect it to.
Punching in / checking out,
And ebbing our way towards another
Draining day.
We're making millions for greedy people
Who don't need it,
And being made to feel like we owe them a favour,
For trudging through each day.
Home with no energy to then enjoy
Our own lives and families.
The joy of corporate life.
There's a pension plan at the end of this all.
Apparently.
Feels like we're all checking out,
And losing time.

Alcohol.

That first sip felt so good.
A Vampires deadly kiss,
That would affect you forever.
A relationship that you'd never be allowed to leave,
On your own terms.
That power was never inside you
In the first place.
Those claws grip onto you with a vice like grip,
And now it's come along again,
To claim it's latest victim.
She goes by many names,
But we call her alcohol,
Sweet to the taste but poison to our souls.
She has been greedy with my family over the past few years.
Two Brothers and a Step Father later,
Again, she comes back.
This time for my younger sibling,
Her appetite is phenomenal.
You try to quit her,
But she always wins you back.
Apparently he has 6 months left?
She plans to come back with her best friend.
He wears a black cape,
We call him Death.

Bryson Graham / Drum Legend.

You loved trains that travelled too fast,
Just like your life,
But we were too slow,
For someone like you.
And behind those locks of hair,
Was a Jaguar in despair,
We'd always find you with ice in the blood,
Beating hard on leopard drum skins,
With a gift that gave you demons,
And a darkness from within.
Spooky Tooth & Girl,
An insurmountable world,
That you lived in and gave us the ride,
Of our lives. But what was left behind was a legacy,
And a pathway for us all to remember you by.
Watching you on YouTube made me a fan,
The passion shown by your Nephew Dave
Shows that your star will never fade away.
A giant in the musical world,
And in the spiritual one too.
We will never forget your name,
Bryson Graham. A Lion never tamed.

Rainbows In My Sky.

So if you have a gay friend,
And I have many.
They call it a Bromosexual Friendship?
Never understood why everything,
Needs to have a label. Is it to make people
More universally accepted,
Or is it the media exploiting
Another crude way to make the headlines?
I have gay and lesbian friends.
They are the rainbows in my sky.
The God Fathers of my two beautiful Sons.
I am glad that my Sons will grow up,
In a world that accepts only peace and love.
This gives them every chance to live,
Happy and kind lives,
Where everyone they meet will be touched,
By their beauty.
There is beauty in all forms.
Especially in rainbows.

I Bought You a Diamond / You Sold Me a Lie.

The date was meant to be cheap.
Chips wrapped in newspaper,
And a park bench seat.
We had Thunderbird "Wine",
Girl, our night was complete,
And the sounds of the 80's,
Shared between a Sony Walkman.
We wore double demin. Big hair and make-up.
We were barely alive, let alone New Romantics.
Watched Band Aid and a host of the best musicians ever,
To grace this Earth. The aim was to make money for a starving country.
Reality, it paid for arms, and the poor never saw a grain of food.
But we were young, and we'd never even heard of the internet.
I bought you a diamond,
But you sold me a lie,
Because you left me with no peace inside.

Those Tiny Moments.

Those tiny moments of release,
That memory pause
That eventually becomes a clear vision
Of the incoming madness
That serves us a daily plate of life these days.
We use a profile on social media
As a platform to show everyone connected to us
That we are doing better off
Than we really are.
Selfies. Poses. Posts in flashy places. Dinner.
Minor personality dysfunctional details
We left at the login stage.
Dreams of California,
Dreams of becoming the next "Big Thing".
An industry whore, a dreamer.
Without a road map we are no longer guided.
We are bottle necked into the maelstrom of madness,
We burn out too young these days,
Better connect again,
Before it all goes up in smoke,
And we miss that last "Like".
Those minor details,
What the hell happened while we were asleep.

We Went To Vegas.

We didn't throw the game,
We gambled all that we had worked hard for
Over those last 52 weeks of a long year.
We went to Vegas,
And lived "The Dream"!!
Tried to look rich and play alongside
People who were way above our level of finance,
We did crap at the crap tables,
And left with only sand in our shoes,
And a bad sunburn.
Crappy holiday snaps of the desert
And a vastly closed down town by day.
We spent our dollars in under two weeks,
And came back home to another year of underpay
And overtime,
To help line the pockets of the American economy
Once again in the future,
And idiots like Donald Trump…
Whatever happened to intelligence was lost
When a confused country elected this modern day Hitler.
And then blamed the rest of the world for their mistake.

We Write Poems, You Shoot Guns.

Daesh. ISIS. Islamic State of Ignorance.
Child murderers and the cult of headchopping,
Mass murder and rape. Cowards and cheap shotters.
Car bombers. Goat fuckers. Wimps. Confused
religious Zealots.
The wish of Sharia Law, and the intelligence of a
fucking rocking horse.
The London Bridge attack and the bomb killer in
Manchester.
Targeting a kid's concert and killing innocent people,
Makes you a disease that needs wiping out now!
I know Muslims and they are embarrassed that you
have cheapened their peaceful religion.
Shame on you. Shame on our weak government
Who continuously let you people in,
And fall under the radar.
Give you a big house. Benefits.
All the while the real heroes are our fallen soldiers,
Living on the streets begging for a handout to eat.
Was 9/11 really a conspiracy?
Can we ever trust the sight of a white van man
again?
We write poems, you shoot guns,
A faceless enemy because you don't stand and fight
like men,
You throw a bomb and run.

Lost Dreams.

While we were staring at the sun,
Holding ice cream hands,
Our inner thoughts melted away,
Just like our dreams,
That only seemed like yesterday,
As we looked into each other's eyes,
And realised that all the love we felt for one another,
Would soon come to an end,
We danced around on marshmallow feet,
And drove each other around the bend,
I felt the sorrow and the pain,
When you finally left my side,
And now I'm flying to the moon,
Because I've no place left to hide,
You're in my heart, you're in my soul,
And I still need you so much,
As I've got no place left to go,
I only want to feel your touch,
Yet, as I fall into another dimension,
And still thinking of the past,
I hope that one day I'll be back,
And find true loving that will last.

We found it all so simple once.
I love the way the media and caffeine
Can screw with you. I feel sad for the former me
From the 1980's. It's a good job that Ferris Bueller
Had his day off and is probably now a beautiful corpse
With a Porsche wrapped around him
Like a metal coffin. We lived way too fast back in the electric era.
Luckily most of us made it through.
The 42 year old me is smug in the knowledge
Knowing that I made it through the madness
And is now enjoying a generation of selfies and people
Who just cannot tear their mobile phones
Out of their hands. Wait a second?
Don't we all do that these days
Without actually realising it?

Life fizzles out like the last firework
In the display.
Leaving us without the brightness
We felt all those years ago
When we were young,
And with hopes and dreams
Still fresh in our minds.
Teenage aspirations and plans of world domination.
That togetherness and energy
We no longer have.
We grow old and tired.
Our bodies worn out

From a long journey and many experiences.
And all that we take to the grave
Is a worn out shell. A shadow of our
Former selves. We say goodbye.
Our journey now over.

This year I published a book.
King of the Sunset Strip.
281 pages long. A great amount of content.
Put it out there for sale.
On Amazon. Paperback and Kindle.
For a great price too.
Everyone said they'd buy it right?
Leave a good review for me,
Help me along the way as a new artist.
Get my name known around the poetry community.
So far I have given out 10 books for free.
Ordered another 10 books.
A few friends have stuck true to their words,
Ordered and left a review.
Most people just want me to hand it to them,
Signed. Oh and for free.
It's not as if I am going to make my millions on this deal,
By the way.
 It seems like we live in a time
Where we hate to part with the purse.
So the next 10 books I send out,
Will be the last 10 books I send out.
Everything must go!
The free book shop is about to close.

So my eldest Son asked me what I had
Written on my T-Shirt the other day.
I told him it said "Heroin". He asked me what that
was.
So I told him it was the name of a brilliant song
From a brilliant artist called Lou Reed.
He asked me who Lou Reed was,
I told him God. He said to me,
"So if Lou Reed is God, is David Bowie
Still the Starman?"
He's only 5 years old. He has class already.
Those proud parent moments,
That you sometimes get.

Ever looked at someone
And you just knew
You would be friends forever,
Partners in crime. Ever looked at someone
And you just knew
That they saved your life and without them you'd be
lost.
I found you at a late stage
In my life
When all was lost
But you helped me fill the void.
I found you at the best stage
In my life
A time when I needed you the most.
I found you
And I hope I never lose you.

Chablis. Popcorn.
A Clockwork Orange.
Retro night, sifting through memories
Whilst dreaming of a digital world
And missing the 1980's.
The Audi Quattro, Rubix Cubes and Pacman,
The New Romatics and a sense
Of togetherness that we will never experience again.
Time has moved on,
Technology has leapt through
The realms of science
Yet we remain at a loss
For an era that helped shape us as Human Beings.
Beyond and into the internet era,
A world where you can have 5000 "friends",
Yet know nobody at all.
We sipped Gin Martini's
While watching the ocean roll in on itself,
Not realising that it would be the very last time
That we saw each other again.
You told me that you had a secret,
A subtle way of telling me that you were
Slowly dying and that this would be
Our very last sunset together,
As we parted, your handshake was stronger
Then any other,
Your hug was harder and lasted longer
Then ever before.
You had tears in your eyes and I laughed,
I called you silly and that I'd be seeing you

Within two weeks for a BBQ and Bourbon,
Once again you smiled.
You told me that you loved me,
Once again I laughed.
A week later you were gone.
You left no note. Just my broken heart.

We walked away from our fortune.
We were stars man?!
We were the main event
Not just willing to plough through life
Like a side show
With no opening act.
Days of grace finally over.
2012 and our summer was over
Before it had even started.
A phone call while I was at Heathrow Airport.
Awaiting a life changing interview
For a new job that would have set me up for life.
An interview I'd never make it to.
The news of a suicide. My older brother Wayne.
2 months shy of the birth of our 1st Son Cooper.
We had a 4D scan of the baby the day before.
It was the Saturday before Mother's Day.
He wanted to know the sex of the baby,
And that everything was going well.
I sent him the scan picture late that night.
Next day, Sunday, Mother's Day 2012,
A day I will never forget.
His team Chelsea were playing.
Had a few too many drinks,

And then made a very bad decision,
One that destroyed all of our lives,
And ended his own. Such a waste.
A bright light burnt out way too young.
1974-2012. 38 years of life over
With the swing of a rope.
Way too young to die.
I will always ask that question, Why??

Bourbon Street.

Dreams of grandeur,
A soul shaker,
A street with no name,
Call me an undertaker,
A legend without a clue,
And a demon in your view,
Another line stolen from Poe,
I really can't be confused,

An urban legend, or a dream of dying,
Can't stop showing my middle finger,
This is my act of defiance,
A kiss in the dark, or a silent voice,
I really don't care,
Take a pick – it's your choice,

I didn't start the fire,
I only supplied the match,
Like a transmitted disease,
Or other bad things you could catch,

There's Bourbon Street, and a view up ahead,
You could be a passer by,
Either way you'll wind up dead!

Tennessee.

yeah right,
I got a feeling inside,
Can't get it right,
When I think about you,
I cannot sleep at night,
The only place I want to see,
Downtown Tennessee,

Will it make me more a man,
To put my heart on show,
I've tried the best I can,
And still I really don't know,
The only place left here for me,
My Lady, Tennessee,

I know we're never going to meet,
But do I have to live in sin,
As I have promised you Heaven,
And I just don't know where to begin,

There must be something left for me,
My darling, Tennessee,
I've walked through your hills,
I've travelled through the night,
Your constellation of stars,
Telling me I'll be alright,

My baby's waiting there for me,
My beloved, Tennessee.

Drawing In Blood.

You must be a long way,
From home boy,
I can tell from the look in your eyes,
Did you wake up one morning,
And find yourself dead,
In a world that developed black skies,

Did you carry a weight,
Too much for your soul,
In a place where you never belonged,
Were you sent out of town,
To find a new home,
Were you weak when they wanted the strong,

Did you worship a demon,
When they wanted a God,
Did you value the things,
That they all forgot,
Were you drawing in blood,
While they drew in ink,
Did you make too much noise,
When they needed to think,

Now you turn to me,
With your arms open wide,
So do you expect me,
To take you inside,

To show you a world,
Without pain, fear or strife,
You are in the wrong place,
As I can't save your life,

Did you worship a demon,
When they wanted a God,
Did you value the things,
That they all forgot,
Were you drawing in blood,
While they drew in ink,
Did you make too much noise,
When they needed to think.

Lead Me To The River.

This is my voice,
Can I sing you a song,
Won't take me a lifetime,
There's no place I belong,

I'm a victim of sadness,
And a leader of hate,
I feel my life slipping away,
I guess I maybe too late,

Lead me to the river,
Sail my ship away,
Reach for faraway shores,
I guess I'm fading away,

A bounty hunter hiding,
When he should stand proud,
A victim of his own success,
Why shouldn't he speak out aloud,

A memory for my bubble,
That I'm sure is going to burst,
Am I just a jealous man,
As love for me really hurts,
Lead me to the river,
Sail my ship away,
Reach for faraway shores,
I guess I'm fading away,

An orchid floating softly,
So appealing to the eye,
Take me to my Eden,
Or a place I'll never die,

I've cut off all my ties,
Or was it the veins in my throat,
Is this just another story,
Or a suicide note,

Lead me to the river,
Sail my ship away,
Reach for faraway shores,
I guess I'm fading away.

Broken Windows.

We're both looking for the same things,
Are we bred to live in fear,
You played your cards like a magician,
You never fade or disappear,

You made me promise you a Heaven,
Then you put me through Hell,
You hide your love so deep inside,
You made me think you were my girl,

Don't know how much longer,
I can carry on,
I need someone there for me,
Someone to keep me strong,
I'm looking through the costume of disguise,
Your broken windows,
The corpse that's rotting beneath your eyes,

You said in life,
That we were born into shame,
So why this fascination,
When you are calling my name,

They say we learn to love,
What we cannot trust,
So who's fool am I anyway,
Is there nothing left for us,

Don't know how much longer,
I can carry on,
I need someone there for me,
Someone to keep me strong,
I'm looking through the costume of disguise,
Your broken windows,
The corpse that's rotting beneath your eyes.

Demon In My Dreams.

I pledge allegiance,
From the edge of my seat,
From your pretty little eyes,
To your cute little feet,

And when I'm going,
There's a bullet with my name written on,
come and catch me if you can,
I'm always right, never wrong,

There's a demon in my view,
With a smile on its face,
No hearts left here to break,
Just get me out of this place,

Load your weapons and cars,
Place my suitcase in sight,
Help me hide my disgrace,
As I am leaving you tonight,

There's a demon in my dreams,
And my souls open wide,
The time has come to say goodbye,
I'll see you on the other side,

They say the west was won,
With a snigger and a grin,
Too many knives stuck in my back,
To love this life that I am in,

I'm not being cynical,
I am too honest to lie,
Come and take me from this place,
Find me a place I'll never die,

The Devil kisses your left cheek,
Look around as life's a blast,
Like fallen Angels you're unique,
Just like a photo of my past,

In another time and place,
You could be a movie star,
But your star is already fading,
And you don't know who you are,

There's a demon in my dreams,
And my souls open wide,
The time has come to say goodbye,
I'll see you on the other side.

Man With No Name.

I have walked across this land,
Still I bet you don't understand,
What I am and what I do,
But now I'm coming after you,

In your sleep and in your dreams,
As nothing is ever what it seems,
I'm your love and your hate,
No one can stop me it's too late,

Call me from the grave,
Live with me today,
I can take away your pain,
I am the man with no name,

They call me Death - they call me Hell,
And I am coming to your world,
Pay the price – achieve your goal,
As I am coming for your soul,

You can run but never hide,
The Lord of Darkness is by your side,
And I will shame you for your sins,
This is where your nightmare begins.

Beauty In Your Hand.

One of the most beautiful,
Things in a man's life,
Is to get down dirty,
And alone with his Wife,

To be at one with nature,
Come freedom come,
Walking around like a mad man,
Answering questions with a gun,

I'm not insane,
Do I really need help,
Hell yeah!! Love yourself,
Because there's a party going on,
Within this commonwealth,

They're using bombs,
While we use words,
As they are better than weapons,
Damn, this is all so absurd,

Flying planes into large places,
Cowards, bastards with no faces,
Come and meet you maker,
ISIS I'll be your undertaker,

Catch me if you can,
As I can be your Superman,
And I will run along with the hunt,

This is no publicity stunt,

There is a beauty in your hand,
If you can only learn to see,
That life is such a compromise,
And it's taken its toll on me,

I'm not angry, just mad,
And on the off chance often sad,
A time bomb waiting to explode,
But the best friend you've ever had.

Rock Is Dead.

I gotta sing you my song,
Don't know if I'm right,
I know it won't take long,
I'm gonna get you tonight,
Would I be a loser,
If I waved white flags,
Would you call me a loser,
If I slept with…yeah!

Here's a little story,
That I thought I'd never tell,
You promised me Heaven,
But you put me through Hell,
You were the winner,
Yeah, I guess you were right,
But there's still something,
I gotta tell you tonight,

I used to be honest,
You thought I'd never lie,
But I've done bad things,
That I know would make you cry,
You kept putting ideas in my head,

But now I know the truth,
We're all better off dead,

You made me choose,
Between the things I love most,
But choosing is easy,
And now I'm chasing your ghost,

And I'm not feeling bad,
Not even feeling no pain,
There's enough left in this world,
I'll never see you again,
Find me another song to sing,
And I will sing it for you,
The truth is hidden far below,
So why does my heart feel so blue,

I gotta tell you what the wise men say,
They talk of silver and gold,
And myths that never go away,
They live in the mountains,
And they drink from the lakes,
They talk about healing,
And of hearts that never break,

Of future paradise,
And stories left untold,
Of love we'll never find,
And hands we'll never hold,

Because rock is dead,
Rock and roll is dead,
Never answers to the questions,
That are roaming in my head,

People lie and cheat,
Why do they cause us such pain,
And I don't want to be,
Another face in the parade.

Crazy to remember that in the 1990's and early 2000's
We could leave our homes at 7pm on a Friday night,
With a £20 note and go to our smoke filled
Local pubs, play pool, darts,
And have a great night out
Go to work hungover that early Saturday morning,
Start the whole process all over again.
Rice and sweet and sour sauce
On that drunken walk home.
Scratching the door with your key. Eye squinted,
Or falling asleep in the garden,
Smothered in ants.
Then comes Sunday. Call it a lay in.
Meet the boys at 12pm. Watch football.
Roast tatties and salt at the bar,
Leave when the last call comes.
Wake up in the morning
Again hungover,
With an earworm of a song in your head
From bands like Happy Mondays, Stone Roses,
Red Hot Chili Peppers, Gary Numan and Nirvana.
That £20 note made it all the way through
A hectic weekend.
That bus trip was where that note ended.
You woke up with change.
These days £20 is a bottle of wine and some
Cheap pasta and sauce.
Did life become over expensive,
Damn right it did. And some of its shine got lost
Along the wayside too.

You think that your
10 hour work day is over.
You clock out, say your goodbyes,
Pass the exit and head back
To reality. Your norm.
Your comfort zone.
They see you as a manager.
A suit with an easy life.
Upon leaving my first job is to render myself
Useful in a kitchen that's not come back
From last night's pots and pans.
Small mouths to feed.
Prep time. Service.
By the time I actually get to eating my own dinner,
It has gone cold. My hunger gone.
Just the satisfaction of seeing my family eat
Fills the soul with happiness.
A long, hard day from cleaning up after people
Paid more than me
For doing a terrible job.
Walking into each shift as if it's a holiday camp.
7am. Better clock this night crew out.
Leaving me with a disaster to deal with
While trying to do my own job.
And the one these clowns couldn't.

Chris Cornell – Soundgarden.
Black Hole Sun.
The front man from Linkin Park,
The singer of one of my favourite songs
From an era I still love.
In The End – it doesn't really matter, does it?
Chester Bennington. A rich 41 year old with talent.
The love. The hero worship. Fame.
Money more than we'd ever need.
Suicide. Just like Cornell.
Hung from a rope.
The only real tragedy in this is that everyday
Normal families away from the spotlight
Go through the pain of a loved one
Taking their own lives.
Just like my older brother Wayne.
Sad thing is, it is never publicised.
Maybe he was never famous enough.
A millionaire who's career died
Way before he chose to kill himself.
Media? Such an irony. Public ignorance.
Let the social media circus continue
I wonder who remembers this news in 4 weeks time.
Nice one guys. You made the news.
One last time and for all the wrong reasons.
Today we still mourn David Bowie. Says something huh??

The first time
She ever told me that she loved me
I knew it was her way of saying goodbye.
Alone on the platform
And with her,
The train left the station.
And me alone.

We revisit these old graves.
Stories and memories,
Dreams and the lost connections
That we will never again revisit.
An icy warmth surges through us,
Our dreams still within us
And as the passage is clear
We will once more walk that silver mile.

It's been a long 14 hour day.
Back up in 4 hours,
We divide our time in between
What we want
And what we already have
Yet the very best thing
We should wish for
Is time.

Was once a very angry young man,
Differing views on life. Distortion.
Grew up listening to The Doors, Hendrix, Bowie,
Moved onto teenage angst with
Marilyn Manson, Rage Against The Machine

And old skool rap like NWA and Public Enemy.
This music helped shape the way I was at the time,
With views I barely maintain anymore.
I grew up. Had kids. Got married.
Hold down a senior role in a senior company
Have aged quite well but could do with
Minor improvements. Would love to travel more
But am restricted. Bolted to the floor.
Would like to see the world
Instead of four dull walls.
Experience new foods, drinks and
Cultures. Sit on a beach, or outside a log cabin
Reading Charles Bukowski & Orwell's classics.
Have met many people
But haven't really met them at all.
My digital family. Always there but never anywhere.
Eyes without a face.
Was once a very angry young man,
But that changed in time. Life revolves like a door.
Now I'm a middle aged man.
And guess what?
I'm no longer angry anymore.

We moved from table 6 to 61.
The reason? My Son wanted to be outside,
To catch the sun and to flirt with a young Lady.
5 years old with movie star looks already,
This one's a heartbreaker girls.
Blonde hair, blue eyes and a killer smile,
Most people call him gorgeous,
But we only know him as Cooper,

Watching this young boy grow up
Is an amazing feeling,
Makes me feel so proud. Makes me feel young again.
My once cloudy perspective on life,
No longer there. Clarity is an amazing thing.
Once I was a young man,
Just starting my journey in life,
My never ending story rolls along I guess.

My Son ordered fish fingers and chips,
Me a mixed grill, medium rare.
Father and Son dinner date.
The best time of our lives spent together.
I've seen how much I've grown as an adult,
And how much he has too as a 5 year old little boy,
I cherish these moments,
The ones that nobody can take away from us,
I look forward to our future together.

I have a few friends with very
Distorted views on life. They live in a digital age
With digital friends, with digital ideas.
They can travel because they have no children,
No troubles and no responsibility
Other to theirselves and the choosing
Of their next holiday destination.
The sun shines upon them just like the camera
That is always aimed in their direction.
Mile high club morons. Reality queens.
I have to ask myself the question though,
Am I just jealous because I am stuck to the idealistic

Vision of the normal life. The family life.
Weekends no longer the end of the week
When in my youth it was the start of the party,
Now it's a longer day at work with more responsibility,
And the closest I get for a break
Is coming home to cook dinner. Did it all end at only
42 years of age. Are the party days over.
Waiting until 11pm each night to get my chance with the remote control.
An hour to speed date the channels
Before that early morning wake up call?
Do I give my kids the heads up,
Or let them find out about life the hard way.

Lexicon Devil. Darby Crash and The Germs.
Young punk talent washed out way too soon.
It's the punk rock way after all. Underground clubs
In the late 1970's early 1980's punk rock scene,
Broken glass bottle ripped across chest,
Sweaty bars, drunken brawls and cheap booze,
The drugs always came free.
They grew up on Bowie, Iggy, Black Flag, X,
The vocal you could hardly understand
Until put in a book decades later,
And the lyrics were something actually beautiful.
It took that long to discover
And by that time the movement had
Crashed and burned.
These days we have "Talent" shows,
Production line stars and boy bands

That can't even play a musical instrument
Let alone write a lyric. The adulation. The easy way
to fame
And their one hit single,
Written by somebody else, or just another cover
version,
Andy Warhol once stated that
Everybody would be famous for 15 minutes,
In this case I wish he was right,
As thanks to download and not actual sales,
We feed the media machine
That keeps the real musicians off the airwaves,
And these talentless idiots drinking from the gravy
train.

Essentially the hangover
Becomes worse each morning
The older we get.
Is it our bodies way of telling us
To slow down and take better care of it.
Or does everything inside us age like
The outside of us. No longer tolerant
From years of abuse?
Either way this will take until midday
For the eyes to stop stinging,
The head to stop spinning
And for the mind to find clarity again.
This chemical imbalance will only realign
After that first glass of wine at 12pm.
They call it hair of the dog?
I call it an impossible battle to win.

A week off work should be a time
Where you chill out and relax. Get things done
Around the house. Not early wake up calls
From the kids
Spending all day playing Joe the Waiter
To two of the most demanding customers
I will ever have to deal with in my lifetime,
I'm back to work tomorrow and you know what,
I cannot wait to return for some peace and quiet.
Cannot believe I'll be going back
More tired than when I left!

You gave her a kiss,
She gave you an STD,
Modern day love,
No condoms allowed.

I love that you hate me,
Jealous of my life,
And all the time,
That you spend hating me,
You are leaving,
Other people alone,
We finally became equal.

We held a passion
For others.
We constructed plans
To make other people happy,
Although staying miserable
Ourselves.

We smiled.
Yet all we wanted to do,
Was cry.

I love it how men go mad
At how their daughters are treated
In there relationships.
When all along,
They did exactly the same thing,
When they were once young,
But to another mans Daughter.
#Karma…

They called it immoral,
You called it sex,
She was old enough
To hold down a full time job,
And a full time boyfriend.
She smiled and pushed out her chest,
She had titties and a killer smile,
That melted you from the inside and out.
A body you longed to touch,
And a garden that needed to be sewn,
And you longed to sew your seed.

Day off. Ham sandwich with no mustard.
Annoyed that I didn't have something so basic
In my cupboards.
Another case of life always getting in the way.
The sun is out here in Surrey.
Rosé wine but no company,

My youngest fell asleep on me.
I look at my garden.
How I long to put on the BBQ and cut the grass.
Put on some music,
And throw on a steak.
It's times like these
That make the struggle worthwhile.

I asked you to save me,
It wasn't that I was scared
Of how my life was going,
Directions change all the time.
It was because,
Like all of us,
At some stage in our lives,
In this modern era,
We lost the map,
And the Sat Nav won't charge.

The transition
From being a child,
To then having a child,
Is the biggest step change
Anyone will ever go through
In their lives.
I have spent my whole life,
Being selfish.
Always wanting it to be about me.
Now, as a 42 year old man,
Alone and without the two older Brothers
Who helped shape me as the man

That I am today,
I feel kind of silly.
I blamed my parents,
Most was relevant blame.
A broken home as a youth.
A drunken and abusive Father,
Who turned his back on me
When I needed him most,
Yet, I could never see my life any different,
No more nights out,
Just movie nights in with my two little boys,
We build for the next generation,
The process continues.

I left a job to discover
Newer surroundings
And to wipe that slate clean.
It's strange how you can be vilified
For being the best employee
In the building.
I feel sorry for those left behind.
That wire jaw line,
Those superstar teeth,
That sold a billion units of Colgate
And a movie contract,
That earned you millions,
A Vidal Sassoon hairstyle,
The look of the 1980's sit com,
Knots Landing – Corny scripts,
And the sensation that life
Would be so much better

If only we listened and stuck to the original model,
Filo Fax. Porsches, and Kelly LeBrock, Daryll Hannah
And Andi Mc'Dowell.
Weird Science. Back To The Future.
The best movies, the best video games.
Music that defined a generation,
And still does.
We played unafraid in fields and came home
Full of bruises. In those days we called it sport.
Nowadays kids put everything on social media for sympathy,
The age of video text. Emoticons.
Anyone ever noticed that William Devane has a face
For every Emoji. I keep about 300 on my phone.
My friends now share with the joke,
Great actor. Fuck Emojis.
I'll just keep on sending people that big toothy smile
of his.

My two sons have two
Gay Godparents.
A married couple.
A beautiful pair of Human beings,
That I would protect with my life.
I love the fact
We have exposed our two young boys
To ignore the ignorance
In the world that has always been there.
Through race, religion and gender,
I am proud that the children I have helped make,
Will be amazing men

And will add so much class and quality
And intellect and love
Into a dying world.
I love that they see no prejudice and that every relationship
Is formed as love and is ordinary.
No matter what.
I just love that they will grow up
Surrounded by love,
And always feel that love.
This makes me feel so proud.
I've started them on an amazing journey
And adventure. This also makes me proud.

Got this whole writers stuff down to a T.
I spent 10 years suffering,
From writers block.
Started writing at the age of 14
Childish poems, ballads to nobody in particular,
Became prolific. Always carried a little note book
In my back pocket. It followed me everywhere.
I absorbed and learnt every word.
On nights out, I'd play the fool,
The circus master. The clown.
It made girls laugh in the 1990's.
A poem got me my first proper date.
In my later teens I discovered The Doors.
Jim Morrison. Lou Reed. Leonard Cohen and David Bowie.
The writing got darker,

As did my personality. It was always a war
Between the pen and the page.
But I filled volume after volume of folders and pages.
Dark reflections of the world
As I saw it. After a long time away from
Building literal universes,
That beast awoke in me again,
I felt alive again and ready to become active
And write a book. This year I achieved my dream.
The King of the Sunset Strip was released
In June 2017.
My debut. And now the world can be my Judge.

I sat here at 22:45pm
The pizza was cold
The nachos were drying out
Also stale and the salsa
Was reducing,
I was watching A Clockwork Orange,
Drinking Chablis,
Stroking my black and white Tom Cat,
He's name is Fucker.
Imagine that?
Awkward when my 5 year old
Only knows him as that.
But kids are cool
And I digress.
Always raises a chuckle but shouldn't,
As he is a complete dude.
Both the cat and my Son that is.
Sitting there thinking

That a hard life has been worth it,
I regret lots but have learnt even more
From bad decisions, too much alcohol and watching
Two older Brothers destroy their own lives.
I'm alone now except my little family.
It's times like this, sitting in the dark,
Candles aglow and at peace with myself for now,
That will help me survive another today.

We break mirrors,
So as not to see ourselves,
And each fragment
Laid to waste
Is the last image
That we will ever see.

It's great to read
Other people's attempts at poetry.
Their words. Vocabulary.
The things that make them tick.
It's a community for sure,
If you're serious enough about it.
Recently I've met online
Two amazing poets
From across the pond.
They hail from Chicago.
Two different styles.
Angelo Spizzarri. Jason Clay Oneal.
Immense talent. We're all starting on our 2nd books,
Just after our debuts came out
Almost at the same time.

I'm in great company. I feel blessed.
Yet we've never met each other.
The weird thing? Feels like we've known each other
our whole lives.
I have their backs. They watch mine.

00:52am. Long day at work.
Ended just over two hours ago.
A ready meal and the cold shoulder.
Sitting here watching amazing
Psychedelic rock music shows
From the 1960's and of course
Writing this new book,
I love these lonely hours
Which always end up as being your most productive
Hours. No distractions and a daytime
Of experience. Drama.
Material that helps fill a page,
And let that anger out.
I'm wearing a Frank Zappa T-Shirt
And avoiding the yellow snow.

I am just fragments,
Of my own imagination,
This strangulation in life,
Creates it's own devastation,
I'm bound by your rules,
Call it alienation,
I'm not looking for answers,
Just an end to this,
Complication.

The magic,
Is inside
Each and every
One of us,
Do not be scared
It's a normal
Occurrence.

I sent out books
My debut.
Far and wide
Across each corner
Of this world,
Most replied
With gratitude,
Some with a photo,
While others took my offer
And did nothing
To help me promote it.
An unknown author
Self published,
Didn't ask you for money
Just your time.
I footed the bill.
Just wanted to get noticed,
Not ignored.

Never been a fan
Of self promotion,
To me, if you have to
Promote yourself,

It's because you've not made it,
Or you lack talent.
And like minded people
Who are confident
That you can deliver the goods
Every time
Will soon see through
The façade.

It started with the pains
From inside my body.
Small but powerful little jabs
Into the side of my ribs.
Invisible rabbit punches
That led me to walk around
Holding my sides and rubbing them
From time to time.
It wasn't the power of an entity reaching through
From the void of its world
And into our own,
It was the effects of my own self loathing
And chemical dependency
Which was always helping to attack my body.
These daily troubles
Invisible to those who have never
Lived with an addiction.
The constant craving that never leaves you
Throughout the day.
And leaves you drained
Before the night has gone down.
We look at a milky, greedy moon

The face of the lady in the sky
Watching over us sleepily
And greedily. That voice always whispering
In your ear. Do you open another bottle
And awaken feeling drained again,
Do you make the choice to say no,
And maybe buy yourself some more time,
The choice is yours. Alcohol is an unforgiving bride
That you will never leave at the alter,
Unless you see through her lies,
And the destruction it can cause.
As The Clash once sang,
Should I Stay Or Should I Go.

The clouds looked like
Beautiful orbs in the sky,
Like something from
A Stanley Kubrick movie
From the 1970's.
2001: A Space Oddity. A Clockwork Orange.
A beautiful sight
In a poisoned sky.
We gaze up in child like awe,
And watch the world
Pass us by.

Every day
We are pressed to make
Decisions.
Some are essential.
Some are selfish.

Some we are forced to make
Through others greed,
But most are the result
Or others stupidity.
Yet we continue
To make our decisions.
Regardless of their
Consequences to ourselves
And to others lives.

She tried to win him back
With a smile
And a push up bra,
And all the while
She had forgotten
That her body had given up
All its secrets
A very long time ago.

You read the papers
Just to realise how disconnected
We've become from the real world,
The digital age
Has turned everyone
Into Smart phone zombies,
Me included.
I actually miss having to look for someone
If you wanted to find them
And speak to someone face to face.
Technology does have
One defining feature though

Which would be well received in real life.
That ability to either block or delete
Somebody from your lives forever.
Imagine that.

The town freak. The outsider.
He wore a Stetson hat
And a purple suede suit.
Like something from a 70's porn movie.
Red leather shoes and white tweed
Frilly shirt and cravat.
We put him in a category
Because he dared to look different,
Drove a Cadillac and smoked weed,
Listened to George Clinton and the
Parliament of Funk
And had a gold tooth.
We saw him as difference because unlike ourselves,
He had his own style,
Had a family and took the joke as it was intended.
While we walked around
Too scared to express ourselves
For fear of being different.
Yet, deep inside,
We longed to be just like him.
We were caged birds,
But he was free.

I smiled when I saw you
That very last time,
Safe in the knowledge,
That I would see you again
One day.
I awoke
After 10 years dormant
As a writer.
Everything felt fresher
Then before.
The words more crisp
The execution
More clinical
The art form
More sculptured
And the ideas
Fresher than that first dew
Of rain on an autumn morning.
Out of the cocoon
Once again.
Take flight and soar to new heights
And become relevant again.

This guy has some serious
Street smarts dude!
You can tell by the way
He wears that hat
That he must've spent
Over an hour getting ready,
And over £1000 on that suit. And those shoes?
He must be a Lawyer.

You penetrated my mind
With a kaleidoscopic view
Fragments of your world
And visions fed me the knowledge
That today I have attained
And passed onto others
Including my children.
I know times come and go
When your loss is felt on different levels
But knowing that we shared
The same life together
Makes me feel so proud.
I know both of you look over me
And my little family.
Just a shame I couldn't have shared it
With you. Made memories now lost
And good times never shared.
The decay started over 5 years ago
And within 18 months I lost both of you.
Tragically. A suicide. And a death by alcohol.
My two older brothers. My guardian angels.
Now I'm alone. But never alone.
Wish I could hear your voices
One last time.
Just wish that you'd both come back home.

Let's team up,
Entwine our hearts,
Together we could make,
A great tragedy.

The bully sat there
Always in the corner
Of the room.
Hidden and non attentive.
Seeking out his next victim
Angry at all of those people
That he would never become
But always wanted to secretly be.

I gained my inspiration
From people who I thought were great.
John Fante, Charles Bukowski, George Orwell,
Edgar Allan Poe & Jim Morrison just to name a few.
Jack Kerouac and others from the beatnik era.
I read their tales and poems
Of desperation, the depression era,
Of the loss of God and their fight against
Drug and alcohol addiction.
Addictions that almost pushed them
Over the edge. Into another dimension in life.
I saw their struggles, yet didn't learn from them.

It is hard to fight
Against an enemy
That you cannot see
A voice that is
Always there
Whispering in your ear
And taking control
Away from you
Making you choose

The wrong options
And dragging you further
Under those waves
That you can never swim against
We all face our own battles
In life. Our demons.
What's your one called?

February 2018. San Francisco.
The plan to meet another amazing poet
A friend I met on Facebook.
We released our debut books
At the same time with another dude.
He's another kick ass writer too.
We plan to hang out, sit under the bosom
Of the Golden Gate Bridge
Watch the sun go down
While drinking cold wine, eating Lobster
And feeling inspired to write
Some amazing poetry. Set in the after glow
Of the 1960's and 1970's
Alcatraz a haunting view over water
And beautiful landscape. The feel of a movement
Shifting. The streets of San Francisco.
I need to work hard and save for this trip.
I've been there before. Many years ago.
I was a young man who didn't see much
Back then. Now as a middle aged man
Married with children,
I see the world in perfect clarity.
Take a cable car down to Fishermans Wharf, Pier 39,

Pier 70 at Pontero Point. Sip from the cup of culture
And get drunk in the history.
Man we came here to promote our books
And to hang out.
We came to conquer. Conspire.
It's a long flight. I'd better pack my bags
Put on my coat, and close the door
On my way out. I hope she understands.

Need to find a 1960's Ford Mustang
For the journey.
American muscle car. A Shelby GT500.
Jim Morrison owned one once.
Drove it into a lamp post.
So now we find Poets Corner.
The new generation
Trying to become relevant
By copying the older generation.
Instead of a dog eared book
And a worn out notepad
They have an iPad / iPhone
Google and modern technology.
There is no learning anymore
No teachers. Anyone can write a blog
Four word speech
And call theirselves a poet.
The quality is in the end product.
The devil of the detail.
I would rather put out a book
Every 12 months and have credibility
Rather than copy people, have little to no content

And release a tiny pile of shite
Online every 4 weeks.
I guess in life it's all relative.
You get what you pay for.

The 1990's were fun. The end
Of our innocence. Cheesy pop music
Replaced by the Madchester Indie Scene.
Thunderbird wine and nights hanging
Over the park. Stumbling into our first jobs
And adulthood with the ignorance
Of youth to guide us into that new
Scary world. The excessive partying
And falling onto the bus each morning
With red wet eyes and sore heads.
We were young and invincible
Or so we thought. Looking back now
What a learning curve. Most of us
Made it out of those mad times alive,
While others of us
We're not so lucky.
I raise a glass to all those
Dear friends and family of mine
Who didn't quite make it
And who broke on through
To the other side.

That haunting look
In your eyes
Tells me that this is not going
To end well for us both.

Just remember
That some people
Will always try
And doubt you.
They have to
In order to make
Their selves
Feel better.
This has nothing
To do with you
But everything
To do with them.
Their hate is their weakness.
Their sickness.
And eventually
It will consume them.
You will be free.

I often look at older couples
Creaking along the pathways
Ancient relics
Of a long forgotten era
They have fought through
Many decades. Much poverty and war.
Hunched over and holding knarled
Arthritic hands. But still needy for one another,

And still very much in love.
And then I look at people
These days. I feel sad for us all
As we will never experience
That level of human connection.
After all, these days
We are connected to computers
And phones. Humanity finally
Found itself replaced.
Here come the robots.

I think that it was
That last glass of Chardonnay
That finally made my
Mind up.
I would continue to drink on.

Last night in Paris
Knowing that I won't see
This beautiful city
For too much longer
During my life time.
She poured me a drink.
I poured out my heart.
We parted as strangers.
The city and I.
It scares me these days
The lack of talent
Regarding films.
In the 80's we had the best films
The best scripts

The most beautiful women
Best leading actors
Who are still major league today in 2017.
Somebody once said
Talent ages and dies?
I say those ignorant fuckers
Need to cocoon their selves
Away from the Internet
Somewhere on a desert island
And play monopoly. Start to go.
Back to square one, pass jail
And learn to live again without technology.
The lesson is there to be learnt!

The poet stood among
His audience. He didn't see the bullet
Until it passed straight through him.
Dazed and confused
He lay there dying
And began to laugh.

People will always criticise
You for your art.
They said it was meant to be
Constructive. But deep down
You know it was a cheap attack
By someone who was
Just jealous that you had
The talent that they would
Never have. It's just in some
People's nature to act that way.

Writing a poetry book
Is something so personal
As it allows other people
To see deep into your soul.
You take the reader,
Mostly strangers you'll never meet
Into those dark places
That you never knew still existed.
You cut yourself open and dissect
Yourself piece by little piece
And all for the entertainment of others.
You travel to places far and wide within your psyche
Explore Borderline realities.
Re evaluate who you are
And where you are going.

It always humours me
Whenever I see a youngster
Walking around in a Ramones T-Shirt.
Almost to the point
Where I kind of want to
Ask them what their favourite
Ramones song is.
Just imagine the strange, confused look
On their faces.
Completely oblivious
To my question.

Confused
By my question
She asked one
Of her own
That made no sense
Whatsoever.
In reply
I made a lame
Excuse
Closed the door
And we never met again.

I was waiting
For what seemed like
A lifetime.
More delays on every line
Going in and out of London.
While others complained
And sipped cheap coffee
I did what I do best
Plug in my headphones
And start writing a book.
Something tells me
That my day has already been
More productive than others
Around me. They had their moment
But chose to lose it.

A pregnant lady stands
Not because she chose to
But because there were

No available seats
And nobody would give theirs up.
The selfish reality
Of the modern world.
I offered mine immediately.
Not out of courtship
But curtsy. A shame it got to this point.

She passed you her number
You passed her a disease.
Unprotected and unprepared,
She called it a one night stand,
You called the hospital.

Ever noticed
How women have to be
The loudest voice
On a train.
Over pronouncing every word.
Every laugh
A high pitched squeal
And always talking up one another
Like they're the greatest
Thing on the planet.
All of a sudden your phone pings
And the noise almost seems
Deafening to them. The look
Of two ice maidens glaring at you
Because all of a sudden
They have realised that they're not
The only people on the train

And you disturbed their nonchalant chat
About their kids
And daytime television.

We all expire
That is the only bet
We are sure of winning.
We have our highs
We have our lows
We make memories
That proceed us
And by the end of our lives
We hope that we did enough
To make a lasting
Impression on others.
We pay the piper
And depart with a smile.

Soho lost a Legend today
Bernie Katz. The Prince of Soho.
A charismatic 5"0 pocket rocket.
An Icon. I can't make this a long poem
My heart hurts too much.
No more shiny suits. The Groucho Club.
I only met you twice
But every time you made an impression on me.
Feel like I have no right to comment
But you gave me one piece of advice.
And then told me to change my aftershave.
That last text message meant everything.

I saw you from a distance.
You returned my gaze
Walked away
And left me in wonder
Of the mysteries
That you left me with.
I spent a day thinking about you
I'd never even met you before
But you marked me somehow.
I couldn't sleep
I had to see you again
I stalked the train station
Every day at the same time
Always missing you
Making that commute
Into London that little bit harder.
Months went by,
Still I thought about
The girl on the platform
Until one day my train was delayed
Someone had fell onto the tracks
Did she slip or jump?
I knew it was you
But you left me no note.

Our fallen leader
Lay prone on the floor
Smell of chlorine
On his breath
We need a way out
Or a witness to the killings.

While brushing
My teeth
The other morning
I accidentally
Swallowed some toothpaste
The immediate
Reaction to vomit
Is exactly how
Some people make me feel
Upon meeting them.

We looked
Into our futures
Without a crystal ball
And realised
That every turning
Lead to a dead end.

Every corner
I turned along the way
Was like a child
Walking blindly along
A dark corridor.
Never knowing where the final
Destination would lead too.
Yet, I continued along
This path towards
An unknown future
Where one day
We would be left alone
To figure it out for ourselves

To face the world alone
To make decisions
That would alter everything
Within the years to come.
We awaken late at night
Sweat on foreheads
And panic in our minds
We look up upon an autumn sky
It is here that we see
The face of God.

I watched the rain fall
From the insides of my safe confines
We called it a PJ day
But actually was more of a case
Of not being bothered to venture
Out into the cold.
Both children playing up
And the TV playing mundane cartoons
I won't get to see the remote control
Until the whole family is asleep
I get about an hour to myself alone
Just me and the silence
Skipping through the channels
Skimming through my shows
Like I am speed dating the box.

Left remnants
From a last meal together
We shared the wine
Over pouring each glass

Woke up with sore heads
And vowed to meet again one day
That day never came
As you were always too busy
And I was always too needy
Life always getting in the way.

Cannot think of anything
More frustrating
Than waiting in the barber shop
To get your hair cut
When you have such little
Time left in the day
And the queue is never ending.
The dull décor
Out of date newspapers
And magazines
Mocking you
As out of boredom
You are bound to reach for one
Anyway.
There's always that one guy
Who after sitting in the chair
For over 30 minutes
Wants an extra inch off
And you continue the wait
For your turn. Always smiling
When all you want to do is scream.
Cannot think of a worse way
To waste a day off.
Roll on dinner and wine

This day could still end up great.
And here I am still waiting!

I bought her flowers
Red roses
In the hope
It would make her smile
As when she does that
She can light up a room.

I was made to feel
Selfish for just wanting
One single moment alone
Just an hour to myself
After spending all day and night
After a hard day's work
Caring for everyone else's needs
And not mine.
No "Hi Honey, I'm Home"
Moment for me.
Walk in, jacket off, tie off,
Say hi to the kids
And then spend the next hour or so
Cooking three hungry mouths dinner
When all I wanted to do was say hello
Spend some time together
And maybe sit down myself.
Change out of my work clothes
Pour a drink and talk about our day at work.

Most of us
Act like nothing
Could ever hurt us
We feel invincible
Yet, we don't realise
That in everyone's life
There will always be
An End Game.
A date. An age.
And even now
I'm wondering
What will be my magic number?
Bingo hall death
Served up by a corny old
Seaside entertainer
Famous once inside his head
For 5 minutes back in the 1970's.

Did my first Lesbian wedding this year.
Was an amazing experience
Was an absolute blast
My two young boys
Have learnt to see past diversity
At ages 19 months and 5 years old.
Am glad I could give them that one last gift.
That gift called Acceptance.

The will to juggle
A thousand pieces
Of an imaginary jigsaw puzzle
Before midnight

And an early alarm call
But all you really want to do
Is continue drinking
Gin and elderflower tonic
Listen to Life on Mars
Write some poetry
Maybe even finish a book?
Your little secret
That everybody knows
You are working on.
The next big thing.
King of the Sunset Strip
Volume Two.
Man, in life you pay your dues
You make an impact
Or become a curse.
We are given an open page
To write our history upon.
Some of us can't find a pen
While others
Are too drunk to focus.

I woke up, It was early
03:12am to be precise.
I downloaded an alarm tone
From the Apple Store.
Thought it would help me
Stop being late
And help my career.
Needed to be loud.
Needed to be something

That would be enough
To awaken a comatose soul.
My mind went immediately
To rock music. I needed
A particular sound. I needed to wake up
To a noise loud enough but to me
Sounded like the thrashing
Of Angel wings. I found an old Spooky Tooth LP.
Bryson Graham was the guy
Who hit those skins like his life
Depended on it. I chose that. I loved that.
Each and every morning even today
I wake up to the sound of music.
And it always warms my soul.

It's easy to feel alone
Midnight with a glass of Gin
A computer and a Cat for company.
No TV. No sounds.
Just the purr of a best friend
Who always sits beside you
For better or worse.
I'm trying to write a book man?
New shit. But every word
Is a struggle.
You'd never guess it
Unless you met me.
Can barely keep my mouth shut.

I watch my sleeping child.
The baby. Blonde hair

Perfect blue eyes
And a smile that would make
An Angel blush.
How I long to hold onto him
And tell him that I will
Never ever leave him.
That I will be around forever
To watch over him
And to care for him
Throughout his life.
But that's the thing right?
We know that every single day
Is a blessing. A gift.
We must make each day count
As for as long as we grow
As Human Beings
We are also in decline.
We grind through each day
Working our bodies to the point
Of exhaustion. No machine
Could even compare to our
Living flesh. We grow old
Our values changing all the time
One day this sleeping little boy
Will be sitting where I am right now
And hopefully in a much better place
In life. And I'll be gone.
Life is cruel and love breaks your heart
But as Ian Curtis once writ
Love will tear us apart.

All of your secrets
Die with you
They're the last gift
We refused to leave behind.

We stare under
An opium sky
Void of all
Emotion
As we know that
Everything
We have ever learnt
From the day
We were born
Essentially means nothing
To us in the end.
Knowledge
Not maintained
For any purpose
Once we've expired.
The flowers sent
The poems read
And all of those
Memories spoken about
Us long after
We are all dead.
It was a great send off
We did him proud
Drinks and songs
Sung way too loud.

That long journey home
Is always the longest
After you've been away
For so long. And it feels weird
And as much as you've missed it
Essentially it isn't your home
Anymore. You feel the gravitational pull
To return and recapture
Lost youth. Forgotten memories
And dreams when once we were young
And inexperienced in the journey
Life was about to take us on.
The ones we loved
The ones we lost along the way
For every success and failure
There was that long walk home
That always helped to repair us
And when we grow up and move away
There is still that need but more from loss.
We realise that time has moved on
The parents gone. Siblings gone too.
That front door that protected you
And kept the wolves out
No longer holds that charm.
You no longer hold its key
And will never walk through it again.

That need to blame
Social media
For the problems
You invented yourself

Those insecurities
That control (strangulation)
The constant paranoia
That I am sure will one day
Drive you completely insane
Personally, I'm a big fan
Of social media
It has done many things for me
I've found friends
That I'd lost many years ago
And made new friends
That I wish I knew
Many years ago.
Also this new digital age
That we live in now
Is only dangerous
If you let it take over your life
And become a fake prophet.
It's almost like a competition.
I haven't signed in just yet
Maybe it's my need to not see a page
Full of pouty lips, orange faces and silly looking eyebrows.

We exchanged words
In a heated moment
The colour in your cheeks
Told me that I'd upset your
Fragile feelings.
It was meant as an insult
But you took it as a compliment.

It is hard to fight
Against an enemy
That you cannot see
A voice that is
Always there
Whispering in your ear
And taking control
Away from you.
Making you choose
The wrong options
And dragging you further
Under those waves
That you will never swim against.
We all have our battles
Our demons.
What's your one called?

Love.
Some call it
An experience
While others
Call it
A life sentence.

I decided to chill
Champagne
And make an amazing dinner.
It's difficult
To cook for people
Who have no palate
Or interest

In the finer things
In life.
As I walked back
From the chip shop
I felt cheated.
Eating soggy chips
And a greasy sausage in batter
Wasn't my idea
Of the perfect night in.
We drank champagne
While all the good ingredients
Lay dormant in the fridge.

I was determined
To have at least
One good day at work.
The enthusiasm
I bring to the table
And work ethic
Is second to none.
As I watch lazy co workers
Dredge through their shifts
Doing as little as possible
Sitting in needless meetings
Having unlimited coffee breaks
I feel cheated.
I wear a shirt and tie
And always leave work
Looking like I'm wearing a bin bag
Over myself. I'm called a senior manager
Yet spend all day filling shelves

And working myself to the bone
For a bullish dictator
Always out to get me.
Maybe I should care less
And act like others around me.
But there are always bills to pay
And I still have my standards in life.

I writ a poem
About you last night
Only to be told that
A poem should always rhyme.
I showed you Bukowski,
Dylan Thomas & Edgar Allan Poe.
You didn't understand the words
But enjoyed the story.
I played you some Doors classics
Jim Morrison and his beautiful
Yet brooding doomed voice.
We both agreed that music and literature
Was the elixir of the Gods
And that all forms of Art
In every sense was an amazing thing.
We hit first base
Then fell asleep wearing smiles.

There was a magic in your eyes
And a magic in your thighs
That drove a man crazy.
With a voluptuous chest
That danced like a ballerina

When you walked.
The world knew you as Marilyn Monroe.
Norma Jean was a very, very long way from home.

As if I didn't already
Have the answer
Today totally summed up
How ungrateful
Children are these days.
Thought it'd be nice
To treat the family to lunch.
A decent place
In the town centre.
Service was good.
The kids got paper and crayons
I got burnt sweet potato chips
And a chicken burger
A Mohito, 2 beers and heartburn.
After the 10% service charge
And £80 later
I realised both boys hadn't touched their food.
The eldest complained about the quality
Of the freshly squeezed orange juice
And his posh fish fingers. He is 5.
The youngest turned the OJ down as well.
Oh, and the macaroni cheese
Wasn't to his liking either.
He is 19 months old.
Seems like these days
Everyone is a critic.

There is not much left
Of my youth
For me to cling onto,
So that is exactly
What I do.
I cling onto
Anything I can,
Before it leaves me
Forever.

Recent events in my life
Have made me question
Absolutely everything.
Including my trust in people
Who I thought had my back.
I stand at the very top
Of my profession
Yet it seems like anyone
Can make up a fabrication
And cost me my career.
No questions asked.
Judge. Jury. Executioner.
The Hanged Man card
Played over and over again.

I saw your apartment
The other night
It smelt of alcohol, vomit
And crack whore.
The offer of a frozen pizza
And a shitty vodka cocktail

Did nothing to raise my expectations.
You were in decline
One cheek planted on a cold sidewalk.
I stayed awake
If only to play you The Doors
And read poetry by Charles Bukowski.
I thought you got it
Clearly you were too drunk
To acknowledge me
And the world around us.

We were chased by demons
Every road led to a dead end.
We missed the last train
Back to reality.
It hurt you.
You offered me a blow job
I bought you a coffee.
We parted as strangers
Humming Life on Mars
Making reference
To an Icon
Called David Bowie.
I felt offended.
His legacy deserved better.

We slip in brown stuff all the time.
Be it mud, be it shit.
Some people never really get it.
Funny how one day you can wake up
With a lifetime of achievements

Only to come home
Feeling like an absolute failure.
I've paid my dues.
Been relevant for 23 years
As a senior manager
I met someone recently
Who saw the beast in me. Promoted me
Only to shoot me down in flames.
Everything was taken away
Except one thing. I have a mirror.
My reflection will show a man.
His will show a bully.
I can walk away the better man.
Good luck in replacing me.
I writ a book. You writ a shopping list!

The only people
Out on the roads
This time of the morning
Are Taxi drivers
And roadkill.

You critique my work
You critique my art
But words sometimes destroy
What little joy left
Inside my heart.

This slanging Match
Between us
Is never over.
One of us always wanting
The final word.
Life isn't a game you know?
This is bound to end in tears.
The question is
Who's?

She reminds me of a geisha doll
Without the make up
I look at her and see horror
My best friend just fell in love again.

I have this amazing collection
Of bespoke belts.
Really funky, expensive belts.
Cannot mention any names
Due to copyright
But the guy who makes them
Was a hero of mine once.
Front man of a seminal 1990's band.
Two albums and they disappeared
Yet, I still rated them a lot.
I first saw them on Jules Holland's show
They blew me away. 15 years later
I connected online with the lead singer
He made me 8 belts. Still have them
As they are the most beautifully
Crafted belts I've ever seen.

One day I posted a picture.
A father and son picture. Classy.
He found something in it that offended him.
He threw me an insult. I deleted him.
Never played another song of his since.
Funny thing is that I recently ordered another one
From his website. Two emails passed between us.
Correspondence. Goes to show
That money talks over integrity.
Shame that someone I looked up to turned out to be a twat.

Every page
In this book called life
Leads us to our
Final resting point.
Our destination.
Embrace change always
Embrace life
Never take for granted
The things that you have today
As for tomorrow
It could all be gone.
And in a heartbeat
The minute hand on your clock
Could stop ticking.
Game over.

Never been a fan of spiders
They are the one thing
That creeps me to the bone

It amazes me that
Some people actually keep
Those ugly arachnids as pets.
The actual thought of letting one of them
Walk on my hand
With the knowledge that they could bite you
At any second makes me dizzy.
It makes no real sense at all.

About the Author:

I was born 8th May 1975 in Isleworth, Middlesex (England), the second youngest of four brothers. There was a year between each one of us. We did our own things and lead very different lives. Tragically over the past five years I have lost all three of them. 2012 Wayne commited suicide at 38 years old, and my eldest brother Clint died of alcohol related illness just over a year later, he was 41 years old, my younger brother Spencer lost his fight too with alcohol on 13th October 2017, Friday 13th, the day before what would have been his 41st birthday. I will always miss the three of them more than anything.

This has shaped my path in life differently and has made me appreciate every moment in life, it has also given me the kick up the backside that I needed to publish my work.

For many years I carried around an old folder full of song lyrics and poetry. I had been writing since I was 14 years old, I finally published my first book in June 2017, it is available on Amazon and on Kindle. After releasing my book, King of the Sunset Strip, I started on my first new material in over a decade.
Finally it is here and I hope that you have enjoyed reading it. King of the Sunset Strip: Volume 2 is a brutal read but an honest read that shows flashes of hope along the way, and is the final instalment in the Sunset series.

I live in Woking, Surrey and have two young children and wife Louise, who are my absolute passion in life. Cooper Davies (5) and Carter Davies (19 months old), and two cats called Tiggy (7) and Fucker (6). My other passions are reading Stephen King books and Charles Bukowski poetry, listening to anything from the 1980's, Red Hot Chili Peppers, The Doors and Gary Numan, and films such as Clockwork Orange, 1984 and Taxi Driver.

I live in a complex dimension with an even more complex mind, but it's a fun place to be.

Acknowledgements:

Everybody at some point in their life needs inspiration and I am no different. I would like to just thank a few people who either have inspired me, or, have been there for me in different ways. Alistair Scott-Goddard, Spizz Energi, Gary Numan, Anthony Kiedis and every great musician and story teller I have ever enjoyed during my lifetime.
Lives entwine and love is devine, I hope you all enjoy reading my books.

Book number three is half way finished and will be called: Black Paradise Society: Poems from and Insane Mind, and will be due out just before Christmas 2017.

John Davies. 25th November 2017.

Made in the USA
Columbia, SC
08 December 2017